THE SEEKER

ROBERT W CELY

THE SEEKER

ROBERT W CELY

The Seeker
    by Robert W. Cely

ISBN: 978-1-947844-16-2

Published by Bard and Book Publishing

Table of Contents

Lost

My Name is Lost

The streets are familiar
I know their grids, and crossings, how they wind and where
I am acquainted, well known to their peculiar sights and smells
How the crowds mingle tightest here
And I am lost

This language is my native tongue
These customs all familiar to me
I know the laws that move these streams of human traffic
I know their face
They know mine
Yet I am lost

My family I remember well
The street where I was born, the face of both my mother and father
Their lineage is known to me as well
Americans for more than 200 years on each side
Fought both as patriot and rebel on native soil
And I am the culmination of all my ancestors toil
Yet I remain lost

I am stranger to myself
I do not recognize the face that mirrors mine
These eyes, stare mad and strange back at me, harboring some not quite
forgotten nightmare
These lines creep unfamiliar from the corner of those eyes
The lips move numb and purposeless
And the voice
When it utters forth from that vastless chamber
And the rumble of an alien creature
The den and noise of a species unheard of
It answers to a name I only dimly know
While I wander through familiar places
I know his true name
He knows mine
My name is lost

Adrift

Where is here?
This place mankind woke up and found himself master of
Feeling both alien and familiar
A vague sentiment
Hostile and homely
Plunging through the dark seas of this expanding cosmos
One bright dot of warmth amid a cold expanse stretching forever and
ever
Cold, dark and dead except for here

But where is here?
Adrift as all the rest
Neither sailor nor captain
We are the Earth's cargo, swaddled in ozone
She our womb and vessel
A makeshift mother to our bastard race
This fatherless race of men, adrift on the black waters of space

Requiem for an Age Grown Old

Gone are the children
Who used to play among the city streets
Gone is their laughter
Empty are the places they would meet

Nothing but old men now
And old women, who gather, afraid of all things
No builders or writers or artists
No one left here to dance or sing

It is empty of the sounds of life
The bones of our cities have grown cold
Our glory lies far behind us now
For we are an age grown old

The Brittle Way

There is a brittle way
Walked by vain and pompous men
Born of self conceit and the assurance of nearsighted mothers
Of grasping and infantile hearts
Styled as princes of their kind

It is the way of brittle men
Pale and weak of soul
No mortar or stone to the personality
Men of dining cars and khakis, Pro-Am golf tours and twin outboard
motors
Social climbing wives and raucous craft beer laughter

Fashionable and mirror worthy men
The way of factory made men wed to suburbanite whores
Brittle men of plastic souls
Souls that fade under free sun
And dry rot in the open wind and rain

Tamed

The wild man runs by starlight
In paths time has forgotten
He parts the thick air
And ancient ferns
And midnight blooming flowers

The archaeopteryx flies overhead
The dodo runs beside
In ocean tides he fishes for the coelacanth
And bites the uncooked flesh

By winter snows, white and pale
He hunts the mastodon
In the sultry nights of spring he dances, step-by-step, with the dark elves,
and the light elves, and the Sidhe of the hill

He never treads the empty bogs, lit by the will of the wisp, and full of the
banshee song
Though he creeps up to the dragon lair, until gold bright fire lights the
beacon in his eyes

The wild man runs and the world is his, the Earth his love
By autumn sunset he follows the song of marble halls
In perfumed beds he tastes the mouth of love, the lips of promised bliss
He tries to leave, but one smooth leg wraps around his
"Stay," she says. "Stay with me a while. The mastodon and coelacanth
can wait. The Sidhe will be back tomorrow night."

The wild man rests a night
By day he wears hard shoes and creased pants
He talks in numbers and margins
Deep within, the echoes of starlight fade
And visions of midnight blooming flowers

The Eaters

I see them, waiting
Shadows among shadows
Thirsty as hot stone
Hungry as fire
The smell of rich and fleshy skin, of torpid breath
Wets their mouths, itches their fingers
As do sounds of the hot flush of veins

They stare at nothing and wait
Always pale and hungry
Eyes black and pitiless as poison
Groaning and toothless they take no meat
Lamprey mouths, swollen and grotesque lips
Pale with unnatural lust
Hundreds of sucking probosci quiver in anticipation in their alien mouths
To gorge in Black Mass

What fallen beasts would not touch
They drink:
The blood of unborn heroes
Semen of fathers to be
Sweat of genius
Tears of poetry
Milk of young mothers, torn from their swollen breasts

Limpid and sexless things
They infect prey to make another
Flesh in their own distorted image
Blind, forlorn and hungry
Always hungry
These, the eaters, hunting the highway of brave men
Of dreaming men
Of prophets and seers
Warriors and heroes
A perverse feast, suckling on all that is noble in man
Proud, upright and glorious
This they eat
Gorging on glory to be, unrealized, undone
And make a species unto themselves, hungry as themselves, abomination
like, perverse and twisted
These eaters of man and soul
Consumers of the spirit fire
Where it dies in their dark bellies
Adding hunger to hunger
Malice to malice
Hate to hate
Until we all wander the highways of fallen heroes
Forlorn and shuffling steps
Hunting what walks the earth no more

Unknown

What is man?
But a creature left on the shores of an unknown beach
Whose father let him gently down upon the sands
As the pristine waters gathered at his feet
Waters of a primitive world
A wild world
A world that seethes and roils and rollicks with life
Is sick with life
With an uncontained and bursting life
"Wait here," the father says. "I will return."

What is man?
But the descendent of this bereft child
He has mingled and become one with the wild and teaming life
And on odd hours and in strange fits, when the moon rises, austere and
beautiful on the cold, blue night
He remembers a deep and aching memory, and walks to the beach again
No more pristine and primitive
A modern, graywater beach
And looks over the waves and waits
And wonders when the father will return
And tries to remember, strives to remember
Why we were left here at all

The Dust

Winter comes
Like a holy man who treads among tombstones, mumbling benediction to
the dust
They fall like crumbs
To be eaten by the ant and grasshopper

From the winter comes spring
From death comes life
From the eater comes meat
There is the strong man
And then the dust

The blushing debutante
And then the dust

The laughing child,
The pregnant bride,
The lovesick adolescent

And then the dust, and dust, and dust

Time and I

Time and I were lovers once
Beneath the summer green
Our kisses were the days and hours
To play with and to dream

I followed her along the beach
She danced upon the sands
And spoke to me in foolish tongues
Only lovers understand

We didn't count the passing days
When everyday was free
For Time and I were lovers once
When she was young like me

I fell asleep midsummer night
And woke to find her gone
Empty echoes roamed the halls
Where she had painted songs

The days that she had promised me
Had scattered on the air
I only had her tear drops left
And weaves of silver hair

I saw her on the beach again
She turned away from me
For Time and I were lovers once
Now she is old like me

Meditation

Who can fathom a mystery against the will of God?
Who could pry a secret from those immovable lips?
What could pierce the veil of that ponderous mind?
Or outwit the mind who set the motions of this mad dance,
And knows each turn and pirouette of the atom,
And maps them in his memory,
And thinks each thought of mine as it gestates unspoken and unthought
of?

Of himself
I cannot fathom, or think, or know
Save his will allows me to fathom, or think, or know

Sad Anthem

You smother me with your water
You smother me with your earth
You burn me with your teardrops
And bleed me in your mirth

Oh, and your sad song plays in my ears
Your sad anthem in my ears

I am the wheat that bows in the wind
You are the scythe that cuts my stalk
I long to float on the endless wind
You grind me with endless talk

Oh, and your sad song plays in my ears
Your sad anthem in my ears

But what good are scattered oats?
What garden made with careless hands?
I want to be a friend of the wild earth
You want to make me a civilized man

Oh, and my sad song echoes down the years
My sad anthem down the years

The Godless One

I am the Godless one!
Hear my empty creeds
I bow to none or nothing
Behold my sordid deeds
Right and wrong like potter's clay
I mold for my own ends
What's good today is cursed the next
And only fools contend

I am the Godless one!
I preach the great void
There is none to cling to
All is devoid
Space is cold, earth inflamed
No angels trim the skies
I searched for God, I found him not
He is the great, "I Lie"

I am the Godless one!
Fear ye all who live
Don't barter for forgiveness
I have none to give
Two of your eyes for one of mine
I am the hand of wrath
More blood for blood more death for life
Will be my epitaph

I am the Godless one!
I am the self-made man
There is none I owe allegiance to
Beneath no flag to stand
This castle built by my own hands
With vast and empty halls
A vacant court, I lone preside
The echoes serve my call

I am the Godless one!
I ravage all in sight
There is no food to fill me
My endless appetite
One banquet set, one table long
The flesh and blood devoured
The crimson drink, the carnal feast
All praise the witching hour

I am the Godless one!
The king of all the beasts
A debtor to the father ape
That first climbed from the trees
I eat my fill, I mate and die
One link of endless chain
Survival looms impulse supreme
Luck, our queen who reigns

I am the Godless one!
I only see despair
I only grasp at misery
I only clutch the air
There is no love, there is no hope
There is only death and fear
There is no need for Hell to consume
I have found it here

Conjectures

By the count of the physicist, the universe is four billion years old
A number so great it is nonsense
A Bishop reckoned earth only six thousand
While the Indian says these epochs are but the blinks of Vishnu's
ponderous eye
And our lives do not even irritate the mucus of his lids
These years mean nothing
They cycle on, beyond good and evil
Beyond purpose and doubt

There was no man to count the days when the skies were first born
There is no lineage to trace back, unbroken to that holy day
No instrument was there to measure the wind of each hot breath that
soared from infant stars

Our founding is all conjecture
And yet it makes what class of men we are
The learned and profane
The superstitious and holy
Our conjectures make us
Our conjectures divide us
You are a fool
You are a sinner
Ignorant
Hell bound
Unless your guess is as good as mine

Home Again

Home again
That is a strange place to me now
Everything is too small
Proportions all wrong
The smell of the hallway is not the one I remember
The sounds echo with a strange sort of finality
Like the echoes in a crumbling, ancestral mansion

The mood and light have fled
It is not as bright as I remember
Some shadow has fallen over it in my absence
Carefree joy that pervaded these rooms has dimmed and muted

The shadows of tomorrow have fallen
This is home no more

Dreams of Apocalypse

1

The Savage returns
Born of civilized man, angry for reasons he does not know
Gestated in the womb of TV light
Nursed on the milk of benign neglect and Adderall

He was promised paradise
A place among the stars of Olympus
And the universe would adore him

Dreams of godhood coaxed the stirring id
The dark and hungry id
Dazzled by the promise of five hundred gig divinity
A thousand pixels of immortal essence

At your nod the armies of earth shudder
The virgins bare for you their nakedness
Orgies dance around your starry eyes
And rains of gold spill un-gathered at your feet

Here now! Here it now!
Awake!

The child has become a man
A mere mortal
The elements will not obey
The seas will not clamber
The clouds and the crowds and the busy streets stream unconcerned
No anger
No hatred
Indifferent, they stream and trundle by
Indifferent and unaware
Indifferent to your latent divinity
Not even worth spite
You are but a leaf upon this ocean

If the id would not be a God,
He will be a destroyer
He will wake the Savage from darker spaces in the mind

See him rise
Bitter and ignored
The Savage returns
Born of civilized man
Angry for reasons he knows not

2

The towers rise in smoke
Glass melts like tears
Bulbous tears
Riot teams the city street

The nation cannot hold
Constitutions cannot hold
Law and customs, norms and mores
None can hold
As it disintegrates from within
A world born in fire
Dead in fire
A funeral pyre lit by our own hands
Built by our own hands

Sanity has grown weak
And will no longer hold the madness back
Light flickers within
Too weak to hold the darkness at bay

Madness within
Becomes madness without

Fire and bloody riot
One thousand years of towers rising
To shadow even Babel
Fall to madness and ash

3

Then the quiet
The continents have clambered and sung
Complained, rejoiced, cried in agony and giddy fear

Such noise, a baleful noise
A full and pervasive noise

Even dumb wires buzzed
Machines screamed, the highway screamed
Insistent roars of commerce
Hyperactive screech of industry

The world shook with hive noise
Factory noise, pole to pole
One world, united in noise

Now the quiet
Unheard by any remembered generation

A grave quiet, pale and dead
Falls like the curtain on the stage of Western man
It fills the ears
Dread and pregnant with regret
The quiet of a fallen world

4

Only in quiet can we hear
That subtle noise, the grinding of the earth's bones
The turning of the spheres
The groaning of Titans
Who slumbered beneath the crust as they turn, troubled by morphic
dreams

Those who remain can hear

For the first time, there ears, dulled with vapid noise
Hear the last and testimonial gasp of the passing world

"Man's spirit has grown frail
Too frail to hold his cities up
Too frail for constitutions and societies
Too frail for economics and laws
Too frail for war and peace
Too frail for manifest destiny and coast-to-coast rails
Too frail for industry and invention
Too frail to hold the creative spark
Too frail to hold the fire
To hold the light
By far too frail, by many miles too frail, by ignorance – by willful
ignorance too frail
to hold back the lurking shadow
That festers in each infant heart
And swells in each manly heart
And plots in each womanly heart
The old and young alike
Stuttering and cancerous
Til the soul of man grows brittle
Lethargic and thick with sloth
An apathetic soul which does not guard it's gates
Too weak to be man any longer

<u>5</u>

I smile at Times Square, rich with ivy
The smell of honeysuckle along the interstate
A nest of birds in my desktop
Kudzu on the telephone wire
Rusted shells of automobiles
Where the brown bear sleeps
And the bitch births her litter

I smile at the ocean
Teaming unspoiled with haddock and red snapper
Of pristine oysters
Laughing dolphins
It has swallowed up the skeletal rigs
Eaten the rusted freighters
Eroded, bite by bite, the commercial shorelines and piers
The gambling boats
Seaside Ferris Wheels, it's gaudy lights grown dim

Hurricanes have swallowed the boardwalks
Palm trees reclaim the strips and avenues
Break the black dust of the asphalt terraces and cheap tattoo parlors
The sideshow attractions full of broken promises

I smile at the wild places
Made from urbane streets

Gone are the smells of civilized man
His perfumed gravitas
Canned and plastic air

The scents of earth fill my nostrils
The pine and sycamore
Spruce crowning the hillside
The musty oak, dressed in Spanish Moss
Amphibians swimming through pools of dorovian muck
These muddy smells are smells of strength, hale and ruddy

I smile at the sun
I smile at the wind
I smile at the free herds,
Roaming wild again
Unclaimed and filling the forest

I save my deepest smiles to see my progeny
Sons of my sons
Stronger than me,
Swarthy arms thick and sinewy with muscle
It is good muscle, useful muscle
Not the showroom muscle, oiled and shaved, grotesque and self
worshiped

I see them hunt the distant herds
Huddle about the nighttime fire, telling stories of gods and heroes
They sing together
Fight together
Touch the bosom of earth and drink from her abundance
In simple homes they gather for sleep
In homes dark and full of night
They gather beneath with lusty women
Wives of deep passion
Who by candlelight share tender and violent love
Voluptuous love,
Moaning and breathless

Teeth on flesh
Wetness and hungry mouths
Grasping loins
Thrust of wanting muscle
They share the night and fill the earth with children

Beautiful and mighty sons
Warriors and poets
Singers, dancers and fighters

Lithe and graceful daughters
Radiant as the dawn
Tempestuous and strong as the thunderstorm

I smile for these are my progeny
The nation of my dreams
The earth of my dreams

6

Out of this dead world rises a new and living one
The living world, though it too is besieged by agony
Some new evil awaits in this pristine and reborn world
A shadow reborn,
Made new as man is made new

And the cycle of light and dark rage through the cosmic tides
Each generation seeking out new heroes
If there are heroes to be crowned

Upon this my dream begins
Apocalypse falls when no heroes walk the earth

Man must be reborn to give birth to heroes
Out of new sons the radiant one comes
When heroes walk the earth again
And the shadow trembles

7

It bubbles on these streets today
I see it form
Incubated in these empty hearts
These hearts of frail and pitiful dreams

Brittle fame
Brief and passing pleasures
Weak lovemaking
Uncommitted and formless love
Unremarkable love
Stillborn faith
Airy convictions
Temporary friendships
Unyielding labor
Men without honor
Women without virtue
Children without wonder
Who do not know the ache of father's love, or the bosom of their
mother's affection

A place where dreams and virtues,
Demons and gods
Magic and the shuddering fear of the dark
The night of a billion stars
No more haunt the chambers of the mind

The crumbling stalks
The ending stalks
It draws breathful and near

And we feel it
The chill as it draws close
Everywhere we go
All that we do
With heads down
Huddled against unseen shadows
Against nameless shadows
Waiting for the cold to settle in
Grim and stoic
Waiting for this world to die
Waiting for a world worth dying for

The One Who Matters

Who is the one who matters today?
The man who can say:
Other men praise me
Women want me
The crowds adore me and call my name
They cheer the feats of my body and admire the lines of my figure
Newspaper men talk of me to one another, and wonder what I will do next
Twitter buzzes about me
Rumors gather at my feet like dead leaves
While your children dream one day of being just like me

Behold, I am the man that matters
And though you have made me who I am
You are not
You are my maker
And I your man born god
But I despise you

And for this apostasy,
One day you will slay me
Like Sodom you will consume me in fire, to make me like you
Your idols will crash to make room for new ones
Yet I am always there
The man who matters
And you do not

Avarice

The hoarder wastes himself
He cannot grab it all
He cannot grab enough
There will always be more
Always something else

The hurrier wears himself away
He cannot do it all
He cannot finish it all
There will always be more work
Always something undone

The worrier drains her own heart
There is danger everywhere
She cannot prepare enough
There is always an expected
Always an unseen danger

All lust is wasted life
You cannot love them all
The harem will never be full
Every day a new beauty matures
Unconquered ladies multiply

You are of finite hand
Of finite grasp
You who would hold all
Who would measure the measureless
Who bind the boundless

The Last Night in America

The last night in America
We gathered on the green
The chosen from her streets and gates, the children of her dreams
We had been friends but didn't know it,
Strange people that we saw
Who passed us on the street each day, as hopeless and as lost

From our place high on the hillside
We watched the cities burn
Full of all the wickedness from which we all had taken turn
Some wept for all her glory,
Some wept for all her shame
Some laughed at all the towers roasting across her fabled plains

The last night in America
We sang the old time songs
Of love and life and liberty and times forever gone
No one got drunk that fateful night,
Though we tried our very best
We raised up cups of blood-red wine, and poured out all the rest

We waited for the whistle blow
As the final game was played
In stadiums by candlelight, so who won, no one could say
One last giant pretzel spun
Salted hard as rock
The home team punted, third and two, with time still on the clock

The last night in America
The politicians drank their share
Of scotch and bourbon whiskey, and bitter herbs to spare
But they couldn't stop campaigning
Or promising to bring
A new world from the ashes that had yet to catch the flame

Their best friends stood beside them
The bankers keeping books
While pretty ladies dressed in white shot them dirty looks
And men oiled up in hair gel
Wiped their hands on skinny jeans
And danced to music no one heard in clubs no one could see

The last night in America
The greatest sales were on
"Everything must go!" they said, "before the break of dawn!"
And people lined outside the shops
To buy the things they can't afford
To wrestle for the last flat screen and gamble in the clothing store

Outside the crowded parking lot
A flash mob gathered high
To sing in one discordant voice, "Today is do or die"
We are the people hear our voice
Our will it cannot fail
We shall wait until the sequel films our epic of travail

The last night in America
The TVs all went dark
A silence settled, reigning dead, a muted patriarch
People kept on watching
Bloggers crashed the grid
The twitterverse lit up its rant over what the critics said

Down the shaded avenue
The churches all stood bare
Empty altars, empty pews, and vacant aisles of prayer
The churchmen dumped out all the fonts
And locked the belfry tight
Then sang each Dylan song they knew by spectral candlelight

The last night in America
I walked in paths alone
My guide the distant starlight and moonbeams feebly shone
The water by the river ran
Like blood on broken rocks
Its echoes laughed at me for all that I had gained and lost

I looked for you that night of nights
The night that I could spare
All things I should have said to you, but never would have dared
By then you had long lost yourself
Those things would stay unsaid
And sealed forever on my lips like the last songs of the dead

The last night in America
As dawn approached the sky
We wondered quiet in our hearts if by sunrise we would die
Our monuments lie shattered
Our totems crushed to dust
Our irons towers bowing in the weight of modern rust

We heard the weight of judgement
Bring down its thundered steps
With what would we present the day for all our hours kept
The darkness wouldn't keep us
The daylight burns our eyes
We turn our heads America, the new world on the rise

The Greatest Question

Of all questions
That tug and itch with insistence
None more so than this :
Not, where did we come from
But where did I come from?

In what place were the bricks of my soul fashioned?
In what store house did I wait until the fullness of time brought me to the
shore?
From what place did I travel before I filled the heat of my father's loins?
Before I swelled my mother's womb with insatiable hunger?
Or stirred these atoms with irresistible need ?

Tell me I am no accident
My crafting was not of unintentional hands
That I was dreamed of in a mind that dreamed deliberately
Slipping into stupor
So he could fathom the asymmetry of my soul

Not made regardless of the dark
But mindful of the eternal chasm

Not a victim of what stretches forever
Here instead to fill those places up

Dark with light

Death with life
Emptiness with depth and breadth
Eternity – such dark and roiling seas as eternity
Filled with all that is mortal
Until it is swallowed whole

And there, what shall we find there?
Lost again, or found at last?

Chasing Dreams

I used to dream in daytime
She played at my feet and side
I nursed on her warm milk
And she caressed me in her tide
I only dream at night now
She makes me chase and chase
And laughing as she runs from me
In never ending race

The Seeker

Alone

The moon fades from the morning sky
The last star shines no more with dawn
All the night birds have sought their nests again
And I am all alone

The music of the midnight has fallen silent
Though still those anthems echo in my memory
As I walk the path where by starlight I held your hand
And I am all alone

We danced among the scent of unseen flowers
That only bloom in the shade of the witching hour
And though I still feel your hand upon my cheek
I am all alone

I am a blossom that withers in the dawn
You passed me on the street and did not recognize my face
The moon fades from the morning sky
And I am all alone

Fiddler on Fourth Street

He played a mournful tune
Passing by
They knew him not, for other songs
More dull and tepid filled their minds

With eyes closed
He swayed
Crows feet folded tight
Gray hairs forgot their age

He caressed out magic
With strange powers
Told stories
That soared past the glass towers

A younger man of a younger world
Awoke in me
He listened and remembered
What was lost to memory

The feel of meadows and old forests
Blue rock mountain spires
Herds of auroch in the snow
Winter night by fire

Great glory of life
Drunk from deep wells
Greater glory in death
That ages tell and retell

Younger worlds still slumbered
In the passerby
Who knew him not
While lukewarm songs filled their mind

Sung by vulgar gods
Eater of dreams
Dancing to metal tunes
And music of machines

Commanding long rows
Of law enforced monotony
A tribe of one face and form
And inbred mediocrity

Amid this despair he played
Though heard by few
In every note he uttered truth
As I heard him I knew

He who fashions a thing of beauty
Commits an act of defiance
And he, a bright warrior made
Shined with the sun's brilliance

The Seeker

Who are you?
They ask grumbling in empty towers
Who are you that your words would sting?

I have no mother
I have no father
I was born when the west wind howled in the cold morning
Tempered in the heat of earth
Bound to the raging stars above

Who are you?
They cry stumbling in torn clothes
Who are you that you would call us naked?

I am a dreamer
A seeker
A teller of tales and a weaver of worlds
A seer of the unseen and a prophet of a new world

Who are you?
They weep in dark places
Who are you that you would pierce our milk-white eyes?

I am a destroyer
A harbinger
A horsemen on the red dawn
A bringer of flame
And the rage of uncounted shadows

I have come to tear away your old clothes
To slay you with my words
And pierce your milk-white eyes
And my children will build new cities from your bones

Remember Me

Remember me my love
Remember me
When all the petals fall from the bloom of youth
And my eyes no longer shine with the passion of the earth's first love

Remember me
In summer days
When we laid by the water's edge
And nighttime watched over our love

When I am old
And my eyes yellow and dim
Remember me as you remember you
A child of the earth's first love

Dancing with Devils and Angels

I wait for the breaking hours
As the midnight sadly tolls
And the feast my heart devours
Lays wasted in the cold

And I long for the voice of the master
Come calling down from afar
As we dance with devils and angels
Beneath the pale light of the stars

I heard his voice in the morning
When the sun made all things new
And darkness fled with the warning
As mercies settled like dew

Still, I bear old transgressions
Still, I wear the same scars
Still we dance with devils and angels
Beneath the pale light of the stars

We dance in the grove of the meadows
To the tune of the choir's sad song
Where I see through the valley of shadows
The mountaintop where I belong

And I see the hand stretched out to me
And I hear the voice from afar
Still I dance with devils and angels
Beneath the pale light of the stars

Some dance for new wonders untarnished
Some dance for the progress of man
Some dance for the green of the forest
And some for the Kingdom's great plan

Still I dream of the glories of heaven
Still I sing of things as they are
While I dance with devils and angels
Beneath the pale light of the stars

The Man of Shifting Shadows

He is the man of shifting shadows
A paradox and contradiction
A violation of himself

Today he is the barbarian, seething with savage madness
He spits and fights
And growls guttural obscenities

Tomorrow he wears the tailored suits of urbane men
Tender and highborn
Sparking witty jokes and educated guesses

He forms the complex battles of humanity
The war of light and shadow
That shudders every human heart

He is the sinner and the saint
The pornographer and praiser of God
Husband and adulterer
Tender father and merciless killer
A thief and hero
A slave to fashion and freedman of salient thought

By this he moves among the gears of the world
This shadow of shifting man

The Astronaut

An astronaut flew off one day
Bearing the hope of civilized man
To find the edge of the universe

He soared past the boundary of time
Through the quantum veil
Where the real dissolves away
And ghosts of knowledge flicker in and out of being
Past light and dark
Sound and silence
To the edge of the universe, the boundary of all things

He stood up on the precipice
And looked beyond
Seeing only nothing
Nothing upon nothing

Brokenhearted, he soared back
Returning to what is real
To give his sad report to hopeful man

But his earth was gone
Swallowed up by the progress of hungry light years
Only empty libraries and dead cafés remained
The land and seas dried up
Sunburned and wind burned

Words

My songs are nothing
A gasping for air
The fist that closes on empty air
A bald man combing his hair

I Remember

I remember when the world was young
When the stars and moon were newly hung in the sky
Only the sun was old, a distant but benign patron of happy days
Joy filled my limbs each morning
The dew on the grass made me happy, the smell of the rain, the sound of
nightfall
Every day a secret
A blessed secret
A mystery and a surprise

If I reach for nothing
For nothing else
It is to feel the pleasure of the sun and the morning dew
When I was not empty, but full

There is the Ocean

There is the ocean
Of irresistible tides

There is the leaf
Of unresisting will upon the waves

What is man?
Neither ocean nor leaf

But a creature of the sea
Of will
Though small against the ocean's rage

Today it resists
Tomorrow it drifts on the current

Tomorrow again
And we plumb the darkest depths
And rise again to find new shores

Unanswered

Some questions have no answer
Darkness, unperturbed by light
Formless and naked it marks the boundary of what is here and not
What is blind unto the eyes
Soundless and muted on the ear
Mirthless laughter
Tearless sorrow

There is no Earth to satisfy him
No food to fill
No sight that can amaze his restless heart
There is no lover that can save his passion
Or kisses that will quench his thirsty lips

He too was formless and naked
A boundary and a veil

Abide

Your Spirit, Lord, abides in me
And I abide in you
Whatever else my soul believes
This I know is true

We build
Only to tear down again
Weave
Only to rend the cloth to shreds
We sow furrows in salt
Reap the moaning wind
Read empty pages by the dark of night

The last bloom of spring
Is mowed for summer's grass
Woods where the barefoot boy hunted crawdads by the stream has been
paved over by imminent domain
Smokeless rooms
Hide no secrets
The smell of earth
Buried with the past

The child grows
He does not recognize the man
He dreams
And they slumber like seedlings beneath the snow of regret

When spring will come
When comes the thaw
The child will grow at last
Not into the man of numbers
Now the suited drone, treading the broken highway of despair

He will grow
Into the image of the Father
The god
We slumber and wait
The thaw that comes

Your Spirit, Lord, abides in me
And I abide in you
Whatever else my soul believes
This I know is true

Reflections

There is a powerful sound, like thunder it shakes the mountain top
More powerful is the whisper that shatters the foundations of the earth

Strong is the blow that fractures bone
Stronger is the caress that can break the stony heart

Great is the flash of light, so bright it blinds the eye
Greater still is that dim, flickering flame that shines in a world of
darkness

Terrible are the weapons of war, that drink the blood of innocents
More terrible is a lie shared, slander that rots a nation from within

Glorious are the lords of state, who wear the scepters of earthly power as
the crowd cheers from below
More glorious is one truth spoken, that by it life is given

Mighty is the man who can take the life of another
Mightier is he who gives his own, and tramples even death itself

Great is the victory purchased by a share of enemy blood
Greater still is triumph bought with our own

In life and death the shadows
In light and dark they give
By might and strength we wither
In quiet grace we live

Lament of Moses

Should I be a prophet of a world I shall never see?
What curse is this
To suffer in the wilderness,
Without the rest of promised land?

Only visions will I entertain
A longing, uncertain and pure
As I drive this people
Lead them through the dust
Suffer their scorn and spite
Rebellion and derision
They will despise my face and hate my voice
Question and doubt, insult, deride, sneer and mock

Lead them on, amid angry stares and mutterings
And at the end,
Watch them as they stream among new meadows and groves
Among heavy vineyards and fields thick with harvest
Parched tongues, drinking milk and honey
Watch from the mountaintop, but do not touch
Watch as they gather the inheritance of my suffering

See only from afar
All that I work and strive and wander for
Even when I alone believed
And I alone, shall not receive

For What He Searches

Only in dreams would he speak his secret heart
As he slumbers, his wisdom awakens
The darkened mystery of his being unknown to the morning
It draws the vision of his sacred quest
Unrolls the curtain before his sleeping eyes

The new world, an old world reborn

The cities and streets of the mercantile West crumbling under the dirt of
ancient history
Fearful legends of the modern man – contemptible and self loving
The mirror man
The self made man
Homo Narcissus they call him
A dead-end branch of evolution

It molders in its grave beneath the dreams of the seeker

Morning comes
The mist of the dream dissipates and floats away like banished ghosts
The seeker journeys on – to satisfy a dream of unknown substance
A rumor heard by all
Known by none
A myth and a prophecy

A promise that comes only in dreams
Leaves the morning with faint memories of a new world
And draws the eyes to every next horizon, and compels his feet to each
bend in the road
Once more, he promises again
Once more

Everything Becomes a Memory

Everything becomes a memory
All withers into not
What was green and lovely
Decays into rot

Age stains beauty
Youth takes flight
The runners of the bright afternoon
Limp in the fading light

We count the day tomorrow
Brighter than the past
And mourn the growing moment
We know can never last

But the glory of tomorrow
May never come to be
While all our work of yesterday
Has built eternity

Songs will fall to echo
Dawn to setting sun
But what once was will always be
To never be undone

The Unmade Man

He is of a nation not yet forged
No Constitution frames its laws
No laws make its people
No people make its place

It is an unformed place
Not even fathomed, or conceived
Except in the heart of hopeful men
Of dreaming men
Of free hearts that slumber in the hum of industry
The creator man, shaper of worlds and words, wood and steel
Who fashions temples out of starry vision
And streets and homes from sweat and sunburn

This is his land, his kingdom
This embryonic land
Emerging from the dreams of hopeful men
Who have not fallen under the shadow of despair

Men who seek without rest
Forgers and pilgrims
People of a nation not yet born

Unseen Force That Moves All Things

We are all moved by unseen forces
By strange hands we are led
To unknown places
Places we do not speak of
Nor do we see, or behold with the eyes

We hear, and hear alone
Rumors and rumors of more rumors
Speculations and the dried out musings of old men
Who have passed out of time
Who bear one foot upon the endless dark
Who hear the stranger whisper forgotten secrets

What name might you go by?
Father of the broad wind
Heart of the river's current
Midnight call and fulcrum of my desires

Be a gentle hand
A burn-soothing hand
Heart-ache healing hand

The angry world has led me astray
This strange wood of soul-hungry beasts
I am weary and wounded, a broken thing
Be soft with me
Unseen force that moves all things

Season of Discontent

It is the season of my discontent
Of spoiled dreams
And heartache
Of promises broken by malignant lovers

It is not the season to plant
Nor to plow
Nor pull up
Nor harvest the gleaming corn

It is not the season of rest
Nor travel
Nor industry
Nor filling the void with long and winding songs

It is the season of dissatisfaction
Of restlessness gestating in the marrow of my soul
Eyes darting to the corners
Muscles twitching
Fingers fumble with imagined tools

I nurse the nervous wound inside me
Fed on spoiled dreams
And heartache
And broken promises

It is the season of discontent
Waiting to bear her children

What Greater Guide

The dream will lead me on
When all else fades
And the shadows of tomorrow grow long beneath my feet

What greater guide
When all else falls to pieces
When the soul looks upon the soul and asks
Who lead you on? Who marked your steps?
What song did your heart follow?

Q and A

Would you sing to me of earth and heaven?

There is no song for a heaven of empty and black, cold stars
No song for dirt and grass and withered trees

Would you tell me a story of gods and heroes?

There is nothing to tell of fallen gods, or drunk and bitter heroes

Would you dance for me with the dawn, dance in the light of new day?

We would not dance in gray light or the monotony of a tired morning

Will you paint for me light and shadow, of meadows and oceans and
streams?

We have only black paint, and scorched canvas, and chewed and twisted
bristles

Spin for me a cloth then, of bright and warm colors.

What can we spend of sackcloth, with hands that tremble at the loom?

Can you not carve in marble or clay, or cut a face in wood?

Marble shatters to dust at our feet, the trees we laid low and the clay is
cracked and dried

Is there a dirge in your heart to sing for me then? A hymn of proud and
dead men?

We will bury you then on the broad high hill

Six feet of earth for your head

And there we will place a marker of stone

And write these words for the dead:

Here lies a man
Who found virtue in fear
Wove tales out of sorrow
And songs from the salt of his tears

Vespers

Come from the long-far hillside, where the night falls down on the day,
I hear in the distant valley, the sounds where the children play.
And a heartache that trembles with sadness, weeps with its silent tears.
For I long that the days of my laughter could forever be lingering here.

I dream great things of the distance, a refuge from all of my care,
And I know my heart would be restful, if only I could be there.
But if I were to walk to that hilltop, and survey the wonders around,
That would bring only more longing to be standing on some other ground.

So further I wander and further, through unending field upon field,
And I search for that long-sought horizon where my heart can finally yield.
Like the perpetual luster of autumn, or the sunset that never will fade,
So this longing forever loiters, as if sadness for my heart was made.

Then I close my eyes to the night-time, so only the laughter remains,
And I am alone with this feeling that yearns to savor the pain.
And I silently dream of the meadow, where the children endlessly play,
And the day always dawns on the darkness, on my home in Heaven away.

The Nomad's Way

We Are But Seeds

We are but the seeds
Of deeper selves
That slumber in the ground
Beneath a snow of late winter

While the cold world waits
For buds of a warmer spring
The smooth veneer of youth
Decays from the seed

What is not ground
For festal bread
Is scattered to the furrows
Fated to a slower death

There, sleeping in the bosom of the earth
Fading in arthritic lines
Till a warmer spring
Summon the buds of a deeper self

To touch the sun again
And breathe the air again
Not like the seed
Who carries the burden of death

But festers instead with life
New life, broad life
Like branches spreading to the heavens
And roots drinking from the bosom of the earth

Dust and Ash

You are only dust and ash
For you the whole universe was made

You are but one leaf of a thousand that swirl on the autumn wind
You are the mouth of the raging hurricane

You are the slave of chance, at the mercy of a fickle fortune
You are a king who holds the fate of the world in his hands

You are a moorless vessel, tossed about the hungry waves
You are the unseen force stirring the waters of the deep

When you are empty
You are full

When you die
You will live

When you are lost
You will find yourself at last

You are everything
You are nothing

You are only dust and ash
For you the whole universe was made

In Praise of Restlessness

God, thank you for these restless feet
These eyes, that search each bounding horizon
This mind, ever seeking new depths
Hands that burn to hold new wonders

It is the open road for me
Strange faces
Strange lands
Exotic tongues
Spiced food and dark-hued women
Loud bazaars of fragrant smoke and incense
A winding, shadowed way, the mossy copse
Forgotten altars to unknown gods

May these roads never end
To never turn into familiar streets

Let me find again familiar souls
But never find the day when I should say, "I know this place. These roads
are familiar to me."

In seeking, I find
In wondering I know
Questions hide the answer
In wandering I am home

Were I to Stay

Were I to stay through all the night
With you these hours spent
If morning sun would find me here
Will find me discontent

It is the briefest of the hours
Most precious to the heart
And you can only love me best
Because our paths will part

What vision in the sky above
More treasured by the sight
Than that brief star which blazes high
Then vanishes to night

So this our love, by night enjoyed
A one night love will be
Unspoiled by what the day might bring
And blessed by memory

Walk Lightly

Walk lightly
For you will never pass this way again
This moment, once gone
Will fade like the smile of a girl
Who sees the mark of age upon her face
Or the boy, burnishing to manhood
Stands a helpless vigil
Eyes peering past the chain links
As summer mellows to autumn

Walk lightly
In this place and time
It holds many treasures you will never see
Beloved you will never love
Ecstasy unfulfilled
Walk lightly
And hold my hand
For the earth hurtles through space at 67,000 miles an hour
And we walk over the bounds of eternity in just one step

Untamed

I have slept among the soft fabric of your comfort
Tasted the delights of your flesh
Moaned as you savored mine
I swam drunk in dark, red wine and sounds of mingled bliss
I have smoked these strange herbs
Entwined within your dark limbs
Your lips, poison and life

But tonight I listen for another sound
Another cry begs me to follow
An old night I remember, and magic that has yet to die

Tonight I will leave you on your bed, beneath the cool sheets
I will leave the wine and the herbs
I leave behind the moans and the delicious tastes of ecstasy
I leave behind your brown and lovely skin, taut and entrapping legs

I leave these all behind for tonight another song calls me
A song I can only dimly remember
The howl of the Sidhe in the winter moon
And flowers that bloom in midnight

Gift of Fire and Song

<u>1</u>

Behold the Herald of Heaven
On this lone, clear night
I fall to thee in faint and spell
Your oracle
The tongues of thy utterance

Hear! You child of earth
Hear! You sons of man
Hear! Daughters of the peerless sky

Open your mouth and receive
Like holy food
This gift of fire and song

<u>2</u>

It was forged in no furnace, divine or man made
Nor lit by spark
Nor stolen by totem-light of Olympus

Breath-born by one cold whisper of God
And the light house of the soul blazed in a form of dust
King of all that walked the earth
Divine in form and fashion
In blood - a beast
Mating, feeding
Corrupt and decay

Within, the fire rages
Holy fire, holy light, life of immortal man
Life beyond life
The heat of all passion
Imagination of poets
Guide of kings
Strength of nations and empires
Comfort to the lost and despairing
Polaris of the soul
Knowledge of God
Knowledge of self
Knowledge of earth and heaven

Wisdom of the ages - light and dark
Full sun of generation
Conviction of faith
Steel of integrity
Fuel of all endurance that fails not til the end
Heart of sacrificial soldier
Joy of martyrs
Rapture of lovers
Blaze of mother's plundering affection
Warmth of father's rest
Truth and beauty
Grace and peace
All goodness
All greatness
Friendship, dignity, memory
Hope that will not fade
Hope beyond the dark - unconquered by this generation of the apathetic mass
And the formless of the void
Holy fire, life of immortal man

<u>3</u>

If we could move the earth
With what power would we compel the seasons and the winds?
Is destiny ours?
Are we hers?
Do the seasons and the winds compel us?

Do we mate by the cycles of the moon?
Are we drawn to plummet as a mass into the sound?
Or sleep by the warm sands of spring?
Are we king or subject?
Engine or tide?

If we could only hear
As the early man heard
When flowers, still wet with dew of first dawn
Opened and turned their face to the peeling light of heaven

Clear as the single call of a trumpet
Or howl of the grey and frosty wolf
Or cry of the circling hawk
Or in the hungry roar of a wave
Or the salient stroke of lightning
Or the tremble of thunder
Or sigh of a night-bound moth
Or burrow of the ceaseless ant through dark tunnels in the sand

That one sound, the very Song of God
The dance of every atom
Fire of each mordant flame
Spiral of the wind
Currents of the deep where pale fish swim blind and eyeless
Rivers of melted rock and steel - fiery as the blood of earth
Tide, storm, eruption and eclipse
Swirl of galaxies and pulse of dark matter

For to bind all things in harmony
That all creation would dance to the song of her Lord and King

Lost to us, Eternal Song
By so many degrees fallen
Lost to us that music
Which would bear us all to harmony
Perfect harmony with our God and King

One note remains in the deaf heart of man
One resilient sound to bind our souls to his

Seek, it says
And stir the restless heart
Seek me out, the Song again
In all places and seasons
From mountaintop to dead valley and deeper still
From wild place to civic hall
In holy and profane places - chapels, sanctuaries, totems and altars,
brothels and thieves den
In song and dance
In sculpted stone
Poem and story
Seek out, and seek again
In law and custom
In words of forgotten wise men

In laughing feast
In weeping fast
In hate and war
Cold love and soul-burning lust
Death and life
Generation and destruction
Search, and then search still
Through all that is life and all that is death

Obey the hungriness of the song, the desperate thirst
The final note that echoes through the soul
Search until your feet are sunburned
Eyes dim from staring down the fixed horizon
Search and search still
Seek, knock, ask
Cry out on your knees

4

This gift, of fire and song
Last behest to mankind
From God given
May it guide our ever-fearful, unsure and trembling steps on these
precipitous sands
As we march through this dark and unfolding vale of eternity
Be with us, fire and song

Til our searchings are no more
Til seeking has grown weary and full
And that last horizon gives away no more into the distance
But opens to that land of no horizon
Where all roads converge
All paths meet
All feet tread to each other, toe to toe
In that fateful city
Where you and I and all our children dance as one
In time with the stars of heaven

Death Makes Everything Beautiful

In eulogy, ordinary men are rebirthed as heroes
Villains had their moment too

No friend is more dear than the parted
No visitor more fond than he who knocks no more

In recalling, a distant lovers touch thrills all over again
Faded flowers haunt the memory with ghost aromas
An empty chair seems the throne of kings

Death makes everything beautiful
Only the living are cheap
And a thousand moments present worth one that is gone forever

The Grouper and Sardine

The mind of the young
Is like the sardine
It darts with silver streaks
Fast
Too fast to see
It swims the shallows in bursting schools
And the froths

The world loves the young
For it is like them
Shallow and silver quick
Together they are snared in a net
By hasty fishermen
Eaten by the fistful
Half-dozen in one child's mouth

The mind of the old
Is like the grouper
It ponders
Slow
In green, shadowed depths
Swimming amid ancient shipwrecks
And coral beds ten thousand years old

He is too slow
His mind lumbers
He doesn't swarm after fashion
By a hook he is snared alone
By patient fishermen who love the sea
And his body
Served as a feast
At a banquet of kings and princes

Remembered Kisses

I remember them all
Your kisses of deceit and deliverance
Upon my lips
And upon my brow
In sweaty bars
And scented harems
Stolen in wayward alleys, along forgotten streets
In cities whose name no man recalls

To Be Unbound

To be unbound
To sip at the ocean of true freedom
Is the un-wished for wish
The fabric of every dream
The cry of lament
The sigh of regret

With it we mount vehicles that follow the beat of the heart
And follow no law, of land or nature
It is every dream, every forgotten wish that says
If only I could

The God Within

There is a god that dwells within me
He is a little god
Petulant and temperamental

Once he was the lord of plastic men and wooden beasts
His cosmos reached from fence to fence
His cries summoned creatures who lifted him up and fed him and soothed
him until he was a happy god again

Today the fence is gone, and the stars make him afraid
Plastic and wood take on flesh and frighten him even more
His cries are silent and withdrawn, the sullen cries of a forgotten god
Who can summon no creature
Whose world will not obey him

The Enemy Within

There is an enemy within me
He gnaws at my roots
He poisons my blood
A servant to the little god
He stands just so,
Even though he is small, he blocks out the light

"It is dark," he says
"You see, it is dark
There is no light or hope, there is no joy or truth
All is death and decay
Ugly death and decay"

Sobbing, he takes my hand and leads me to sunken and filthy places
There is no food there, so he feeds me dust and rock
Others gather round with fake smiles and hollow laughs
And speak blasphemy to one another

I shrivel in the dark
The enemy nods and says
"This is the way of all flesh
And you are naught but of mortal bone"

This Moment

This moment is eternal
If I but hold my breath, it would last forever
Here, between the pause of two seconds
In a gasp
In the widening eyes of wonder
In a young girl's sigh
In a heartsick pulse of love
Here on the wind
In one moment
In one beat of the hummingbird's heart
The water drops and the moment passes
And I walk again in time

To Those Who Walked Before Me and Those Who Follow

I walk past the steps of those who have walked before me
Since I was aware of steps
Since first I looked upon the sands and saw them
The footprints tracing up the beach
Wandering somewhere up ahead
Far back, they peeled off from the common herd
Where the tourists gather by the water
And eat ice cream
And dance, shirtless and half drunk
Over and over these dull and light prints trace over each other
And the tide washes them away

But these steps, those I follow
Few and bold
Peel away from the safety of the bay
I track them up the hillsides and down to hidden coves
Through old shipwrecks
And the bleached bones of ancient sea monsters washed up on shore
By caves of thirsty pirates and hungry cannibal tribes
Past Charbides, past Sirenes,
Past the Lotus Eaters, past the dark fires of Circe, smelling of incense and
swine
Even to the shores of drowsy Lethe
Strong and deep they tread, undimmed by the tide of centuries
I follow the steps through light and dark, joy and despair
Knowing to God they must go

But here they end
These footprints of mighty men
They are gone, their journey over
Before me, the sands lengthen and the day still burns
There is no more path
No more prints to follow
Only mine will mark the passage beyond

May they be deep and true
May they resist the restless tides
So you, what traveler may come after, and follow these, my steps, further
along the beach
May they bring you closer to the end
And know that, as the steps of men and minds before me
As they stood behind me and with me

These stand with you
To guide and to strengthen your heart
If they say nothing else to you, hear them say:

Here is the way
Walk and hope
One day we may reach the end
And as we have guided you, may you carry us

Sitting At The Well of Souls

Sitting at the well of souls
I watch the colors
Like bubbles, drifting from a depth that even darkness cannot plumb
A place beyond darkness
Beyond light
Past even the genesis of movement and form
Substance and being
Past the boundary where shifting chaos guards the birthplace of brother
cosmos

But here before me, they float from the dim water
Colors that have no name
Born from beyond all things
What rapture they give
What joy their drifting imparts

I reach out to touch
An unseen wind pulls them away
Down the road
Between the tall, autumn trees
Off to be born
In the loins of man
Or in the spark of ideas
Generated in one thrust of fertile inspiration

Or a dancing ghost that will always play in the avenues of the sun
Happy to be forever free

Listening to Rain

I listened to the rain tonight
It filled my heart with delight
And a joy in just the hearing

I watched the stars slow and lonely turn
In the cold of night they burned
Unbothered and uncaring

Little laughter down the hall
Holds my broken heart in thrall
With no effort to endear me

Birdsong in the backyard tree
Given to me pure and free
Without worry or fearing

Just one moment, just one glance
An un-asked for spark of chance
Love for the sorrow, life for the living
Joy for the sake of the gift and the giving

The Hero's Prayer

If I should perish on this mountaintop
The hateful world swarming at my feet
Alone I stand, in conviction
Alone, consecrated for this holy hour

If I should fall by the instruments of my enemies
Cut down by a thousand words of indifference
If my bones should be swallowed by the earth again
And no man remember the place where I have fallen

If I should fight for men
Who hate my fight
Free those souls
Who despise liberty
Give light to they
Who love the dark
And celebrate with joy the longest night

Should this be me
A broken hero
If I should fall among tragic sands
Derided and unsung

At least, my God
Let me live and die by these few words:

May my heart be true
My faith unwavering
My hope undying
And my love as pure as the rains of spring

Do Worlds Grow Old

Do worlds grow old as men do?
Do they age?
Lose their strength? Their sight? Their hearing?
Does the blood of planets grow cold?
Do their sands weaken? Soils wither and fade?
Does the strength of their years palsy as the heavens above pass further
and further away?
Do they die as men? Cough and breathe their last?
Do the people live on, as the ground beneath grows cold?
When the flower blooms no more
And the fig tree gives no fruit?
Do they live on and wonder, what has become of life?

Can it be born again?
Must it die first?

Then let death come
Let us dance the funeral march of this age
Let us play the dirge
Let us sing the Requiem
Let us walk together to the grave, and bury her, fist by fist of dirt
And write her elegy in the temple of fallen races

The Nomad's Way

Sunrise to sunset
Night of the forlorn crescent moon
Across the ceaseless sands
Winds the nomads way

It is the way of ceaseless wonders
Unhindered by nascent thoughts
Unbordered by walls
Yielding to neither law nor custom

It searches monuments of forgotten races
Obelisk's full of glory that move the world no more
Totems to fallen gods
Through shipwrecks filled with sand
By faded alters
In the shadow of trees that have watched the ceaseless turn of centuries

By starlight and sun
Through pale winter storms
In dancing with the thunder strokes of summer

It lingers beyond all caste of men
It circles them all
By cities of the sweaty factory man
Who work in the shadows of the young urbane
Of craft beer prostitutes
And espresso debutantes
Of silicone whores
And one-hundred forty character philosophers

By the primitive world still untouched by progress
Of stone and leather races
Men of fire
Women, blue painted

Further still, through pristine jungles
Unsailed seas
Infant islands
Mountaintops still forming

Deeper through lightless caverns
Past blind and groping worms who sip stalagmite water

Deeper and darker
Where form and void have just met
To fiery, cthonic places
Down the stairway of the world
To foundations that sit upon the pillars of the dark

Round up the path winds
Back into the light, and up again
Beyond the wind, beyond spheres without a name
In heights where play the philosophers music
Songs wise men cannot hear
But heard by poets
Melodies to which the stars of heaven dance

Through temples of airy spirits
Councils of ponderous gods
Asteroids floating by, bearing chained titans wracked on cosmic rock
Beyond the cold, celestial prisons

Who is worthy of this road?
Who would walk the paths of heaven and hell, of earth and sky?

Only he who would walk
He, who would journey untired
He, who would seek no end
Nor end to seek
Whose life is discontent
Whose rest is brief

In that path is life
As boundless as the God it serves
Unfolding, step by weary step, the rapture of the world

Let me walk them all
See them all
Experience them all

Spare me only the stagnant men
The stagnant places
Cities and walls and temples of men who will not move
Who say, "Here we are
Here we will stay
Let us make a monument to our stillness"

Can I make a philosophy of motion?

We are bred for discontent
Without monsters we will make our own

And if I rest
For weary will I grow
Rest while the eon turns into another
Only to wake under a new millennium and find the road again

For who can search out that which is eternal?
Who can find the infinite?

May I be as unbound as the endless sea
May my steps be as eternal as the author of the eternal
And may I never weary of the steps
Or of finding
Or new horizons
New wonders
Ancient and infant
Each new day an unexplored wonder

Home Again

A day, now two, now three
Of unfamiliar places
New sights
New horizons
Skies strange and waves foaming in foreign waters
Then, that road I know so well beneath my feet again
Customs welcome me like worn-out friends
That old man - I see him everyday here - picking up the leaves one by
one

Familiar scents fill me
A house that knows my name
Little ones that call me their own

Tonight I am the guest of honor
They talk of all I missed, of all that changed
These walls, these scents, these arms embrace me and rejoice that I
stretch my feet out by the fire

I am home again
Until travel calls me to sleep beneath passing hospitality
And makes this worn-out place new again

But tonight I rest
Among those who love me best

www.ingramcontent.com/pod-product-compliance
Lightning Source LLC
Chambersburg PA
CBHW020452100426
42813CB00031B/3340/J